MAKING THE GRADE · pREPARATORY GRADE

EASY POPULAR PIECES FOR YOUNG PIANISTS. SELECTED AND ARRANGED BY LYNDA FRITH

Exclusive Distributors:
Hal Leonard Europe Limited
Distribution Centre, Newmarket Road,
Bury St Edmunds, Suffolk IP33 3YB

This book © Copyright 1991 Chester Music
ISBN: 978-0-7119-2525-0
Order No. CH59246

Cover designed by Pemberton & Whitefoord.
Typeset by Capital Setters Limited.
Printed in the EU

Chester Music

INTRODUCTION

This collection of 25 popular tunes has been carefully arranged and graded to provide attractive teaching repertoire for young pianists. New concepts and techniques are introduced progressively, and the familiarity of the material will stimulate pupils' enthusiasm and encourage their practice. The standard of the pieces progresses from beginner to Associated Board Preparatory Grade.

CONTENTS

Ode To Joy	3	
Little Brown Jug	4	
My Old Man's A Dustman	5	
Trumpet Voluntary	6	
Twinkle Twinkle Little Star	7	
Kum Ba Yah	8	
I'd Like To Teach The World To Sing	9	
Humoresque	10	
My Eyes Are Dim	12	
What Shall We Do With The Drunken Sailor?	13	
The Bare Necessities	14	
Top Of The World	15	
Hi De Hi Holiday Rock	16	

Birdie Song	18
Eight Days A Week	19
Supercalifragilisticexpialidocious	20
Ferry 'Cross The Mersey	21
Postman Pat	22
We All Stand Together	23
While Shepherds Watched	24
Hey Jude	25
The Bear Went Over The Mountain	26
Blowin' In The Wind	28
Y Viva Espana	30
Uptown Girl	32

ODE TO JOY

by Ludwig van Beethoven

This famous tune is played by the right hand only.

Remember to play on the tips of your fingers.

LITTLE BROWN JUG

Traditional

The left hand begins this piece, but be sure to have
your right hand ready to play before you start.

MY OLD MAN'S A DUSTMAN

by J.P. Long, E. Mayne & A. Le Fre

There are a lot of repeated notes here, so you will need to count very carefully.

TRUMPET VOLUNTARY

by Jeremiah Clarke

Have your right hand ready before you start, and play
loudly and firmly like a trumpet.

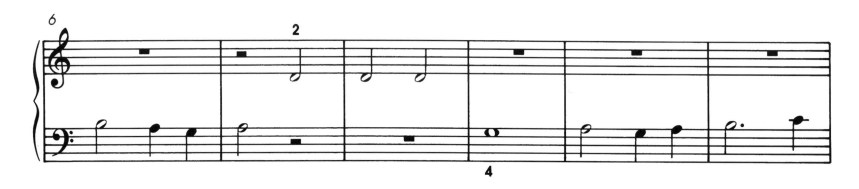

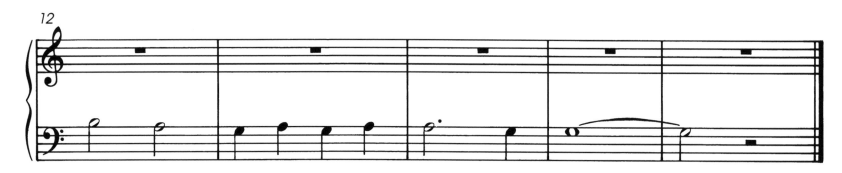

TWINKLE TWINKLE LITTLE STAR

Nursery Rhyme

When you have learned to play this piece, why not try playing it an octave higher?

KUM BA YAH

Folk Song

This piece comes from Africa. It is the tune of a prayer,
so try to play it quietly and smoothly.

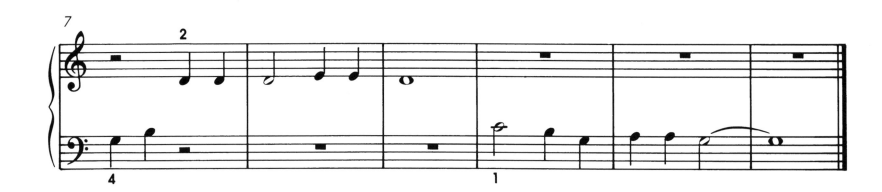

I'D LIKE TO TEACH THE WORLD TO SING

by Roger Cook, Roger Greenaway, Billy Backer & Billy Davis

Notice the repeat sign [𝄇]. Remember to jump over
the first time bar [¹.————] when you play the repeat.

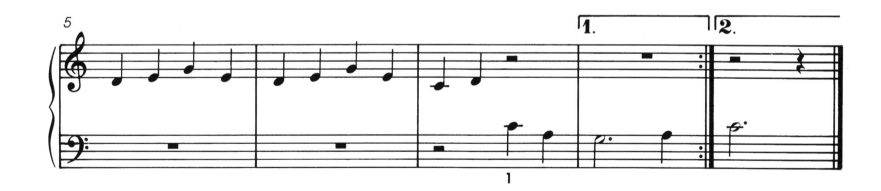

HUMORESQUE

by Antonin Dvořák

This famous piece should be played smoothly and quite fast,
so you will have to count quickly as well.

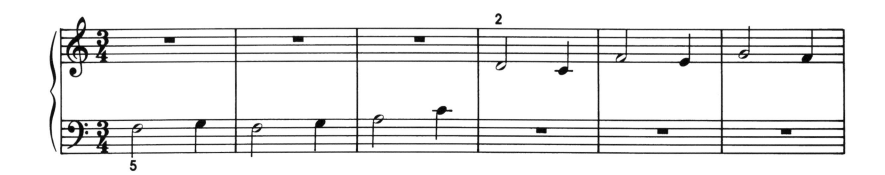

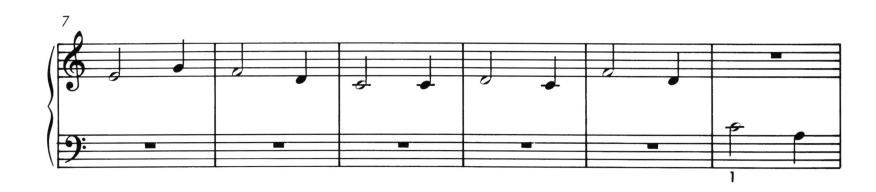

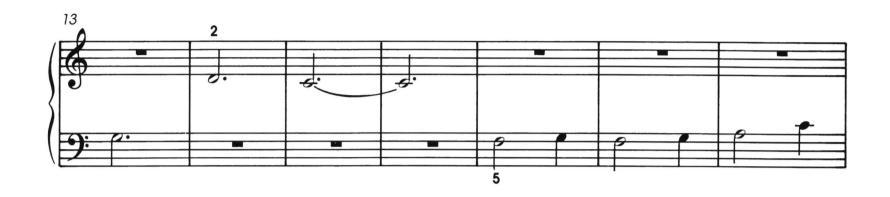

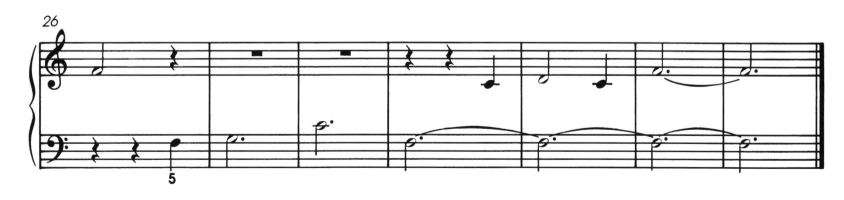

MY EYES ARE DIM

by Elton Box, Desmond Cox & Bert Reed

This tune has some quavers in it, and starts on the fourth beat of the bar.

Count aloud and clap the rhythm before you try to play it.

WHAT SHALL WE DO
WITH THE DRUNKEN SAILOR?

Traditional

Before you try to play the piece practise the first bar

several times, with a relaxed wrist and clear rhythm.

Notice the key signature – all the Fs are sharp.

THE BARE NECESSITIES

by Terry Gilkyson

There are two places, marked by *, where both hands have a rest at the same time.

Remember to count for these rests just as carefully as you count for the notes.

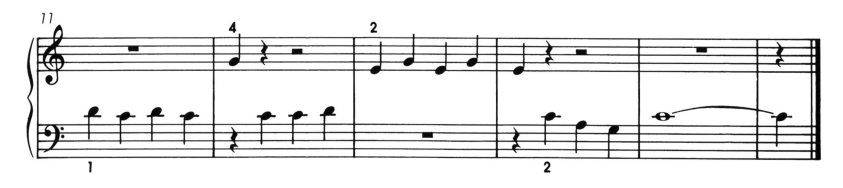

TOP OF THE WORLD

by Richard Carpenter

Rests in both hands again. Look out for the F sharp in bar 10,
and remember that the F on the fourth beat will be sharp as well.

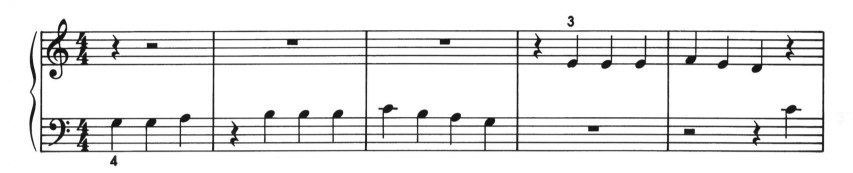

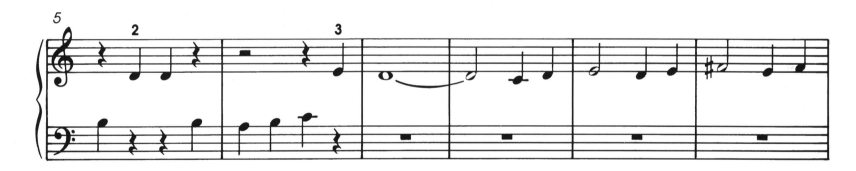

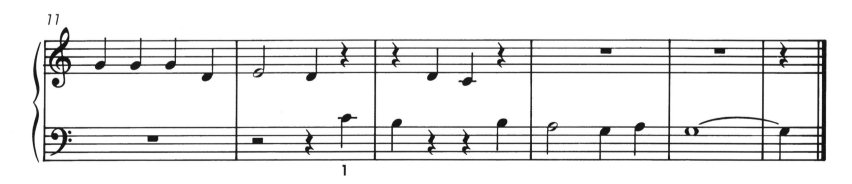

HI DE HI HOLIDAY ROCK

by Jimmy Perry

The key signature is B flat, which means the piece is in the key

of F and all the Bs will be flat.

Look out too for the E flat in the right hand and some A flats in the left.

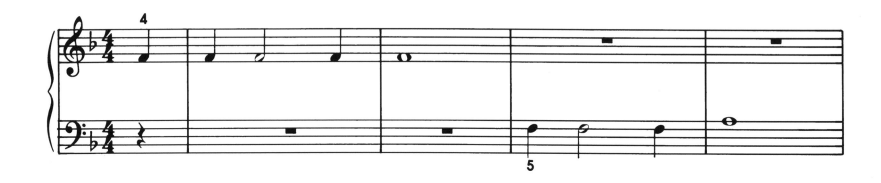

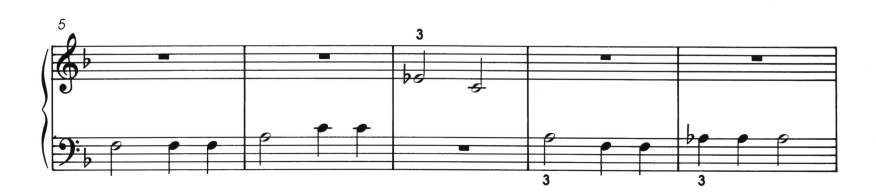

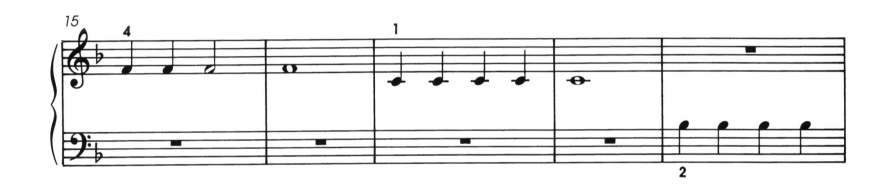

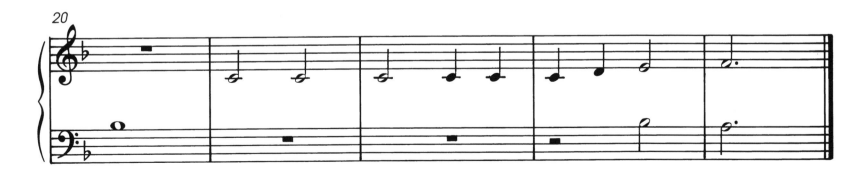

BIRDIE SONG

by Werner Thomas & Terry Rendall

Make the quavers clear and even. Remember that all the Fs are sharp, and make sure
you skip over the first time bars when you play the repeat.

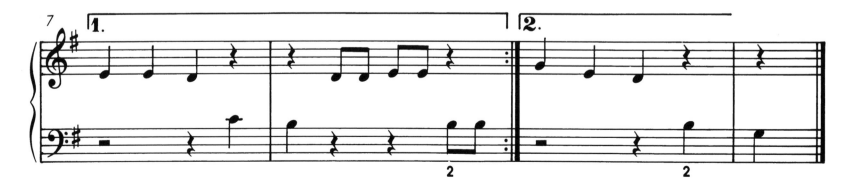

EIGHT DAYS A WEEK

by John Lennon & Paul McCartney

Here the right hand starts in a new position, with the thumb on E instead of Middle C.

Notice the letters '*mf*' at the beginning. What do they tell you?

SUPERCALIFRAGILISTICEXPIALIDOCIOUS

by Richard M. Sherman & Robert B. Sherman

In the left hand the little finger starts on the C an octave below Middle C.

At * the right hand has to move up to another position.

Practise this move before you begin the piece.

FERRY 'CROSS THE MERSEY

by Gerard Marsden

This piece is about a famous ferry in Liverpool. Play it fairly quietly (**mp**).

Be careful to count through the minim rests in the right hand.

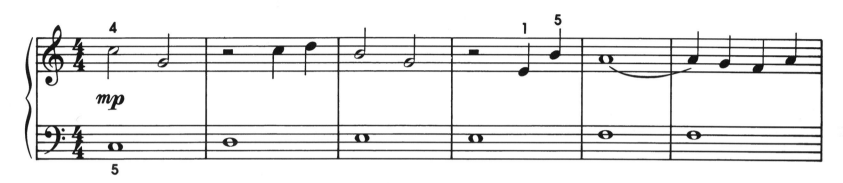

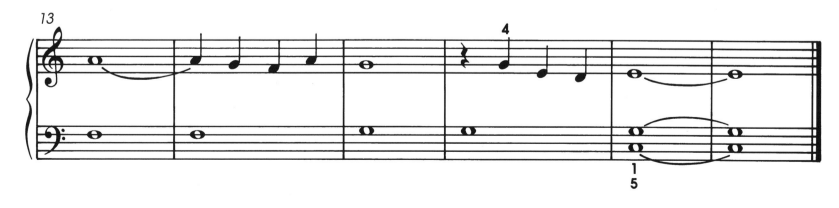

POSTMAN PAT

by Brian Daly

In bar four there is a special symbol 𝄐. This is called a pause sign,

and tells you to hold the note under the pause for a little extra time.

Notice the phrase marks (slurs) in the right hand.

WE ALL STAND TOGETHER

by Paul McCartney

The word 'Gently' appears at the beginning of the piece. Keep this in mind as you play, and notice the signs ⸺ and ⸺, which tell you to get louder then softer.

WHILE SHEPHERDS WATCHED

Traditional

In this well-known carol the right hand has to play the note B below Middle C.
Practise the bar where this happens (bar six) carefully, putting the
second finger over the top of the thumb as marked.

Peacefully

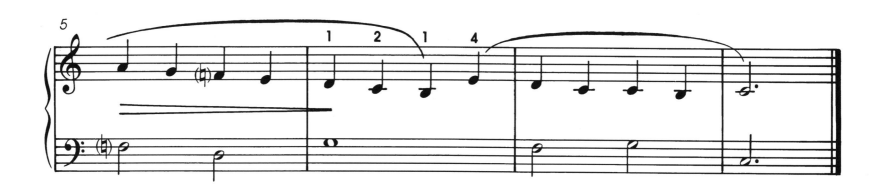

HEY JUDE

by John Lennon & Paul McCartney

At the end of bar four in the right hand, be sure to pass the thumb under
the second finger to take the hand up to the new position.
Bar 10 is a bit tricky, and worth special practice.

Not too fast

THE BEAR WENT OVER THE MOUNTAIN

American Folk Song

You may know this tune as 'For He's A Jolly Good Fellow'.

Make the phrasing very clear, and look out for the pause sign near the end.

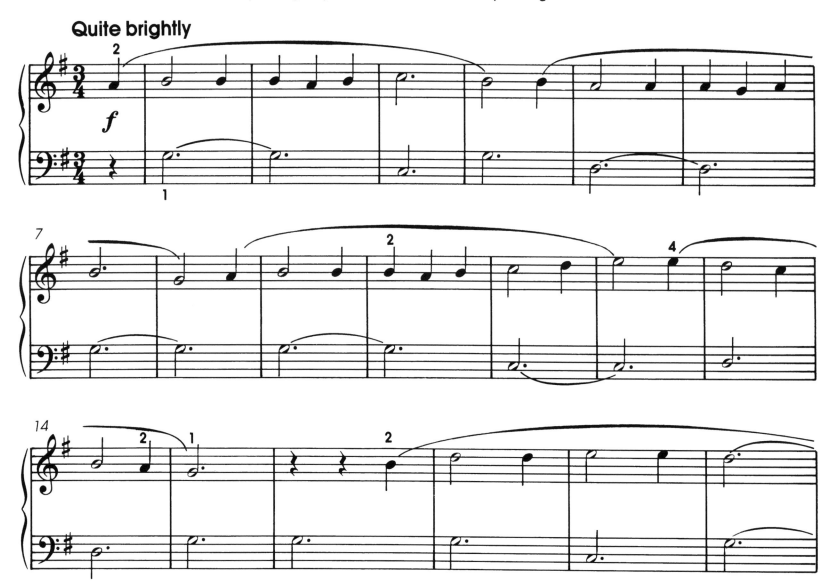

26

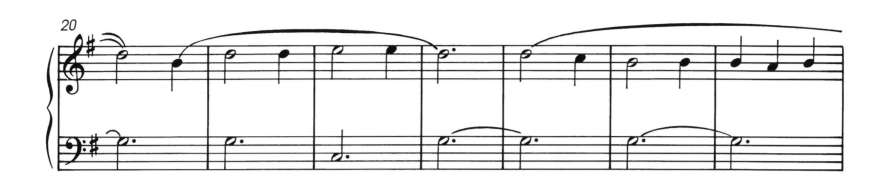

BLOWIN' IN THE WIND

by Bob Dylan

Look at bar three. After playing G with the right hand 4th finger you have to
stretch the 3rd finger down to E, missing out the F.
This happens in three places in the piece, marked by the sign ＼.

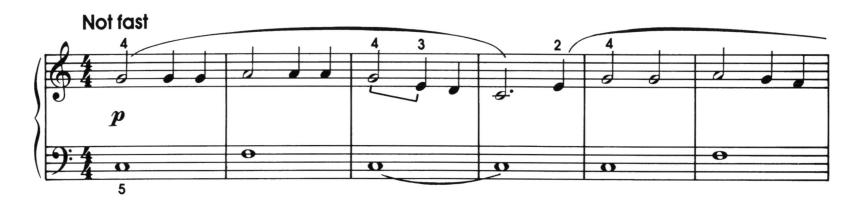

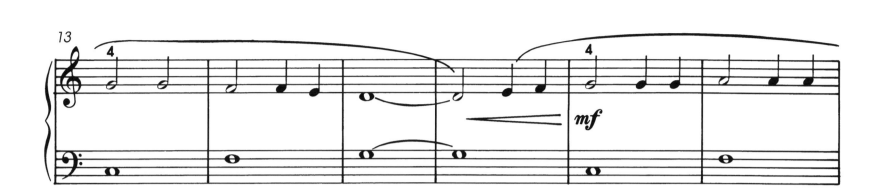

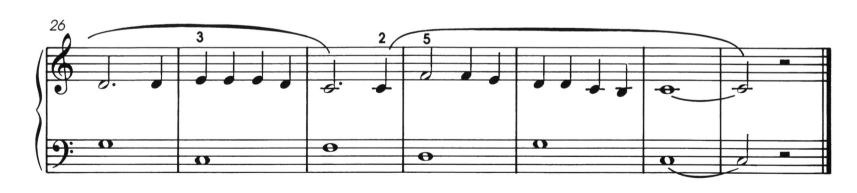

Y VIVA ESPANA

by Leo Caerts

This is a very happy tune about holidays in Spain.

Try to make it sound lively and full of fun

– but watch out for the E flats at the end.

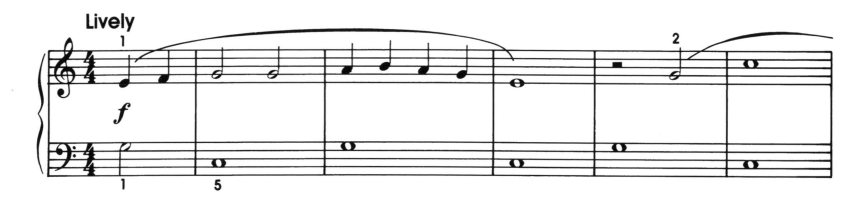

30

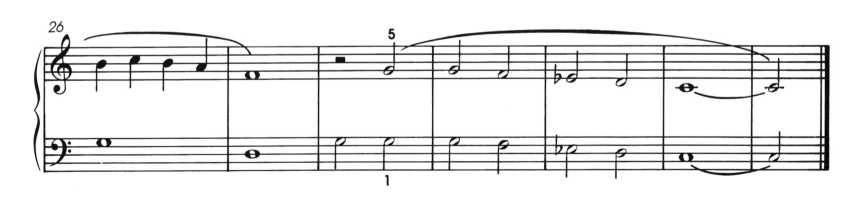

UPTOWN GIRL

by Billy Joel

The right hand has a lot of quavers which go quite quickly, so it would be a good
idea to practise the right hand on its own until you are really sure of it.

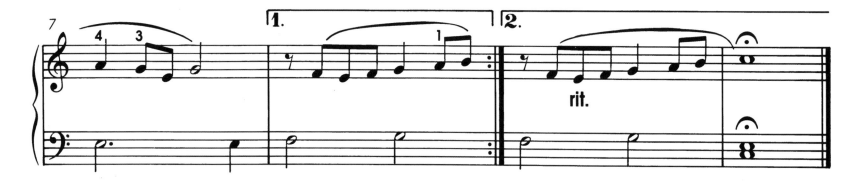